PORTRAIT
OF A
GOLFAHOLIC

MARK OMAN

Illustrations by

A THOUGHT FACTORY BOOK

COLUMBUS BOOKS
LONDON

Text copyright © 1984 Mark Oman
Illustrations copyright © 1984 Gary Patterson

First published in Great Britain in 1985 by
Columbus Books
Devonshire House, 29 Elmfield Road, Bromley, Kent
BR1 1LT

Published by arrangement with the Thought Factory
P.O. Box 5515, Sherman Oaks, CA 91413

Printed and bound in Great Britain by
R. J. Acford, Chichester, Sussex

ISBN 0 86287 196 4

For Michael Cole, without whose unrepentant golfaholism I would never have learned the real meaning of that immortal phrase: "Walk softly and carry a big cleek!"

A PRAYER
FOR DIVINE
INTERVENTION

Now I lay thy club
  to ball
I pray the hole thy
  ball will fall
If I should die lacking
  one last hack at it
I pray the Lord will
  take a whack at it
But if thy Lord should
  somehow blow it
I've seen your club
  O God, don't throw it!

CONTENTS

FORE-WARNED IS FORE-ARMED!

If someone you love has a golfing problem, this book will provide you with facts about the illness and the long road to recovery.

Before this book was written, golfaholics had tried to control their golfing on their own and, only after repeated unsuccessful efforts at such control, finally admitted that they were powerless over golf. At first they could not imagine life without it; they certainly did not want to admit that they were golfaholics. But with the help of this book and GOLFAHOLICS ANONYMOUS, they learned there was a whole new fairway to salvation!

We in GOLFAHOLICS ANONYMOUS know what it is to be addicted to golf and unable to keep promises made to ourselves and others that we will stop teeing off at any time, any place.

Which is why truly caring friends and lovers should give this book to the golfaholics in their life. In fact, we heartily suggest that copies be given to anyone who has ever taken club in hand!

FORE-WARNED IS FORE-ARMED

PART I:

Golfaholics—
Undisputed Champions
of the Wrong Stuff,
Any Way You Slice It!

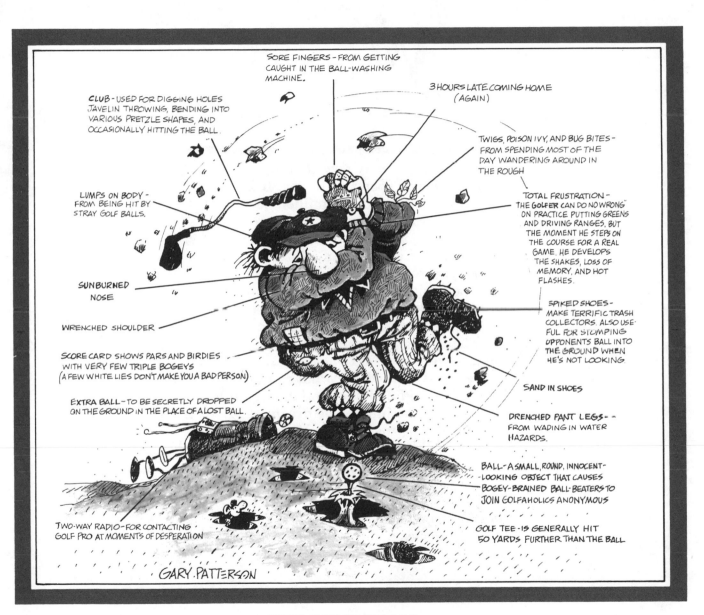

THE GOLFAHOLIC

1
WHAT IS GOLFAHOLISM?

Golfaholism is only now coming into its own as a major sports affliction. It is estimated that nearly 15 million people in the United States alone suffer from problem golfing and golfaholism. This group includes both men and women of all ages.

Today, throughout the world, golfaholism is responsible for untold broken clubs, abused caddies, and battered golf carts.

The price for such carnage is high. Golfaholism costs its afflictees millions of dollars every year in the compulsive pursuit of the latest methodology and equipment designed to aid and abet golfaholics in their addiction to the impossible dream of conquering the maddening game.

Over the years we have learned a great deal about how to identify and arrest golfaholism. Sadly, no one has yet discovered a way to prevent it—primarily because nobody knows exactly why some golfers turn into golfaholics and others never get past fore-play. (But that's another book!)

A MAJOR DEPRESSANT

Even today many casual golfers refuse to believe that golf is a drug. In the beginning it works mostly as a stimulant—players get excited by the prospect of a game and look forward to teeing off. But as they get deeper into dependence, golf becomes a major depressant. Somehow the afflictees' golfing never seems to live up to expectation.

Like other forms of compulsive behavior, for true golfaholics even nine holes are more than they should attempt, yet 18 holes are not enough to satisfy their insatiable craving for humiliation and self-abuse.

The affliction is of such an insidious nature that afflictees often suffer vivid and detailed hallucinations of incredible shot-making exploits—of course these are rarely, if ever, seen by the other golfaholics in the foursome.

As the torment spreads deeper into the mind and putting stroke, these grand illusions are slowly replaced by lapses in memory, sometimes of an entire round of golf.

From here it is only a matter of time before functional disintegration and paranoia take over and the golfaholic's handicap becomes totally out of control.

Our purpose here will be to concentrate on helping those pitiful souls who are already golfaholics so that, in spite of their affliction, they might learn to live relatively happy lives—which is to say the relatives are happy, if not the golfaholics.

If nothing else, we want problem golfers to see what life can be without golf and know it is possible—dreary, hollow, and pointless, but possible!

2
WHAT ARE THE SYMPTOMS?

Not all golfaholics have the same symptoms, but many—at different stages in the illness—show these signs:

They are never content when the round is over. They want "just one more" hole to take away the bad taste of the previous 18. Or they insist on working out their miseries on the putting green hour after hour, oblivious to other plans for the afternoon—like a wedding. Theirs.

. . . OBLIVIOUS TO OTHER PLANS

They look forward to golf outings and think about them during breakfast, at the office, at church, at home, in bed . . .

Golfaholics rarely have large families.

They try to control their golfing by keeping their paraphernalia hidden away at the club and then resort to borrowing other addictees' equipment at the local practice range.

They lie about their handicaps.

They play alone and practice trick shots.

They have blackouts, can't remember kicking their ball out from behind the tree. They'll tell family, friends, and neighbors about their "three" on the tough ninth hole, but forget completely about their "nine" on the easy third hole.

This type of memory lapse has been diagnosed incorrectly as "hysterical amnesia," though in fact, only when they *remember* the nine shots do they get hysterical.

...ONLY WHEN THEY REMEMBER

They become day-old donut junkies and half-cooked Polish dog disciples.

They come home with indigestion, constipation, and double-bogey breath.

They never have enough time to practice—or find enough balls to make up for it!

They find that only when wearing color-coordinated shoes, socks, slacks, shirt, sweater, cap, and glove do they feel on a par with the pros. If they look the part, they can overcome relatively minor inadequacies of talent, ability, and practice and still bask in the limelight as players with the right stuff!

Of course, what we have here are players with all the wrong stuff—and, in some cases, no stuff at all!

3

Is THERE A GOLFAHOLIC IN YOUR LIFE?

Often those closest to a golfaholic find it hardest to admit that someone they care about is a golfaholic. A problem golfer, a duffer, a monumental hacker, YES! But not a golfaholic. The word may have too many disturbing associations for you.

If the problem golfer laughs at the idea that he or she is in trouble with their game, or resents any such suggestions, the following pages may help explain what you can do and what you cannot do. For this book is not based on theory but on experience. We know what you are up against. We know how baffling it is to live with a problem golfer, to see close and loving relationships torn apart by irrational footwork, aggressive hip action, and uncontrollable overswinging.

Above all, we must remember that there is no such thing as being a little bit golfaholic. Once the problem golfer slices, hooks, and shanks over the fence into golfaholism, he is certain to find himself out of bounds, in the streets, and inevitably rolling into the gutter.

IS THERE A GOLFAHOLIC IN YOUR LIFE?

4

ARE *YOU* A GOLFAHOLIC?

To find out, ask yourself the following questions and answer them as honestly as you can.

	YES	NO	PLEAD INSANITY
1. Do you turn away from your regular foursome and seek the company of high handicappers and inferior courses to make your golfing seem better than it is?	☐	☐	☐

	YES	NO	PLEAD INSANITY
2. Have you ever felt shame and depression after golfing?	☐	☐	☐

	YES	NO	PLEAD INSANITY
3. Have you gotten into financial difficulties as a result of golf?	☐	☐	☐

	YES	NO	PLEAD INSANITY
4. Is golf affecting your relationship with your priest, rabbi, or life insurance salesman?	☐	☐	☐

ARE *YOU* A GOLFAHOLIC?

	YES	NO	PLEAD INSANITY
5. Do you *crave* a couple of practice swings at the same time every day?	☐	☐	☐
6. Perhaps a few short shots in the backyard before dinner?	☐	☐	☐
7. And then just a couple more the next morning before work?	☐	☐	☐

		YES	NO	PLEAD INSANITY
8.	Has your house and yard maintenance taken second place to golfing?	☐	☐	☐
9.	Is your house and yard the pigsty of the neighborhood because of uncontrolled golfing?	☐	☐	☐
10.	Have the neighbors petitioned to have your home condemned?	☐	☐	☐

	YES	NO	PLEAD INSANITY
11. Is golfing jeopardizing your miserable job?	☐	☐	☐
12. Do you golf to escape from what's left of a meaningless career?	☐	☐	☐
13. Have you ever discussed your golfing with a doctor—who was not a scratch player or sandbagger?	☐	☐	☐

	YES	NO	PLEAD INSANITY

14. Has your golfing ever caused
you to act as though you
belonged in an institution?

     YES ☐ NO ☐ PLEAD INSANITY ☐

15. Has your golfing ever caused
you to end up in a hospital?

     YES ☐ NO ☐ PLEAD INSANITY ☐

16. Has your golfing ever caused
your best-ball partner to try to
send you to the hospital?

     YES ☐ NO ☐ PLEAD INSANITY ☐

If you answered "YES" to any *one* of the questions, you should take that as a warning that you may be a golfaholic.

If you answered "YES" to any *two*, the chances are that you are a golfaholic.

If you answered "YES" to *three or more*, or Pleaded Insanity even *once*, we're on to you!

And if it hasn't happened already, you will doubtlessly be unemployed within the month, discover your marriage is kaput, be notified by registered mail that your parents have formally disinherited you, and find out your beloved children have become incorrigible tennis brats!

5

THE FOUR STAGES OF GOLFAHOLISM

STAGE 1

At this stage these people may seem to be only weekend golfers. Golfing may be even less frequent and heavy only on occasions.

They may start experimenting with orange and yellow or lime balls or be unduly concerned with compression ratios and dimple pattern—though they will never admit to it.

Their behavior after golf is sometimes embarrassing; yet they resolutely assert that they can handle their golf and that five wretched and blasphemous hours on the course are essential to their well-being and peace of mind as brain surgeons the rest of the week.

At this stage they may be approaching the borderline that separates social swinging from compulsive ball beating.

STAGE 1 GOLFAHOLIC

STAGE 2

At this stage golfers lack control over their ball beating and begin to worry about it. They are unable to stay away from the driving range even when they want to. People in this group often get completely carried away with a false sense of power and flagrantly attempt to slug balls over the driving range fence. They delude themselves into thinking they can continually let out the shaft and swing from the heels and not have to face the consequences of such loose and wanton behavior when they return home.

On the contrary, it is usually the spouse who is suspected of infidelity, while the Stage 2 golfaholic is faithful to only one mistress, a new backswing!

STAGE 2 GOLFAHOLIC

STAGE 3

These golfaholics are desperately in need of help. They truly believe that with enough instruction and practice (for which they are now willing to spend unlimited amounts of time and money) they too can make the journey to Pebble Beach and play the treacherous 18th, and a hell of a lot better than that pro who couldn't take the pressure in the last round of the Crosby and jerked three balls into the Pacific Ocean—which *they* certainly wouldn't have done.

Of course, after actually spending unlimited amounts of time and money preparing for their pilgrimage to Pebble Beach and finally playing the 18th and hitting *four* balls into the Pacific Ocean, they are utterly remorseful and solemnly vow to destroy their tools of the devil and go astray nevermore. . . .

Which lasts for about a week and a half. Or until the so-called reformed golfaholics return home and convince themselves that all they need to make the shots is that new progressive profile antihook antislice set of irons, that classic compression-molded graphite-headed set of woods with extraflexible smooth swinger shafts, three frequency-matched forged wedges, the revolutionary inverted loft toe-connected hatchet-head putter, a dozen big dimpled high trajectory two-tone hot-off-the-head golf balls, new rubber-spiked golf shoes for more gripping power, all-weather leather no-slip

36

STAGE 3 GOLFAHOLIC

glove, and membership in that new outrageously expensive golf club where serious golfers can work on their games in an atmosphere conducive to the sensibilities of one who is truly committed—and should be! For they have now gone past the point of no return.

From here it is only a matter of time before golfaholics lose all interest in the world around them, perhaps even in life itself—which brings us to Stage 4 golfaholics, God help them.

STAGE 4

We are talking real scum of the earth here. Humiliation and wretchedness beyond belief. To all outward appearances, golfaholics at this stage are beyond any sort of help.

By now, they have been on every two-bit muni course within 100 miles, spent long wasted nights at out-of-the-way dilapidated driving ranges with degenerate swingers like themselves, quit every golf club they could afford to join (and most they couldn't afford), and left home and work to experience the sinful pleasures of infamous links around the world, only to return to their loved ones bewitched, bothered, and bewildered, body all achin' and wracked with pain, Saint Peter don't you call them 'cause they can't go, they owe their soul to the country club pro shop—and some 14-year-old hustler at the local pitch and putt!

STAGE 4 GOLFAHOLIC

6
THE GOLFAHOLIC'S PARAPHERNALIA

Those lost souls who really "do golf" make use of paraphernalia that would make a junkie go straight.

And the torturous acts committed with these clubs against one's friends in the heat of battle would surely make the Marquis de Sade roll over on his rack!

For no one else but a loathsome golfaholic would think of using such sadistic devices of the devil as:

THE DREADED DRIVER—A heavy wooden club with a long steel shaft with which to beat an opponent into a blubbering wimp.

THE BAWDY BRASSIE—A smaller wood-headed club, but equipped with a heavy brass plate—all the better to hammer a more hardheaded opponent into begging for mercy.

THE BARBARIC BAFFY—A deceptively small and open-faced wooden bat designed to baffle the enemy with the variety of its fiendish uses.

THE GOLFAHOLIC'S PARAPHERNALIA

THE CANTANKEROUS CLEEK—A long iron-headed stick—difficult to use but an essential weapon in one's arsenal if one is to slay the truly great monsters of golf.

THE MACHIAVELLIAN MASHIE—An iron club that, when used accurately at medium range, can mash the other guy into mush.

THE NEFARIOUS NIBLICK—An iron stick possessing a sinister edge for cutting out the heart of one's adversaries when they least expect it.

THE WICKED WEDGE—A heavy-flanged iron with a large razor blade. Truly great gladiators of golf will use a wedge to decapitate their victims with a single crisp SWISHHHHHHH—dead on target!

Surely the aforementioned, taken as a whole, must constitute cruel and inhuman punishment of the most diabolical dimensions.

But, of course, that is all part of the everlasting lure of the affliction. The very notion of inflicting such sadistic rites on others, knowing full well they will be used against you, only adds a certain sweet and sour masochistic flavor to the proceedings.

And though most golfaholics know the truth, they refuse to face the inevitable:

"They who live by the driver shall die by the wedge."

7

Games Golfaholics Play

One very easy way to tell marginal golfaholics from the lowest of the low is by the particular games they indulge in.

Stroke play is the more acceptable form of competition and is simply one player's total number of strokes against those of another poor devil. All in all, a relatively harmless affair.

And then we have match play, the variations of which can be uncouth in the extreme.

As originally intended, match play is head-to-head combat, one hole at a time. Yes, we're talking a real Sodom and Gomorrah of behavior!

The following represent just a few of the perverted pleasures golfaholics get off on under the guise of match play.

SINGLES MATCH

Also called a *twosome.* Simply two people who enjoy playing around with each other, one on one—though not necessarily on the golf course.

And yes, the old standard "Tea for Two" was originally titled "Tee for Two," a torch song for golfaholics.

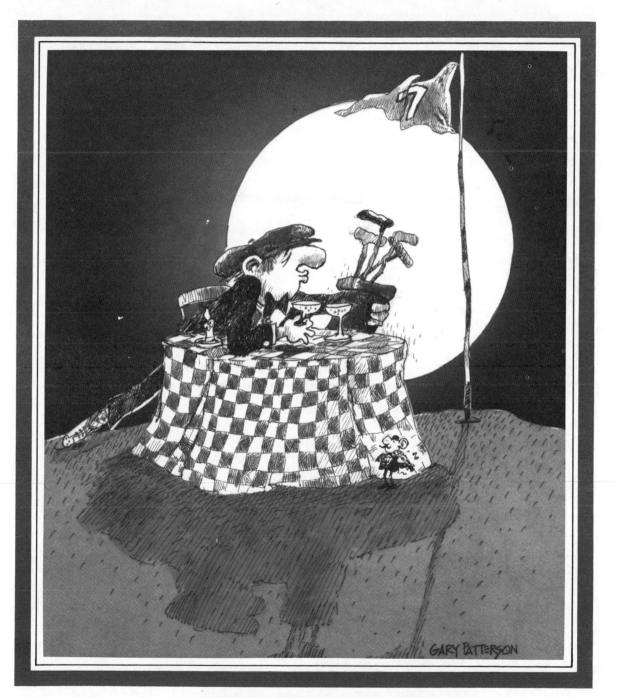

GAMES GOLFAHOLICS PLAY

THREE-BALL

Every man, woman, and gorilla for themselves and against each other, no holds barred. You have to be cunning, unmerciful, and heartless to be a successful three-baller.

FOUR-BALL

Very much like tag-team wrestling only without the honesty, sportsmanship, and politeness of that sport. In four-ball two partners in crime use their best score on each hole to whip the best ball of the other two. Working in pairs provides just enough opportunity for subterfuge, conniving, chicanery, and general underhandedness, to keep true golfaholics coming back for more.

MIXED FOUR-BALL

The same as above except men and women playing together, which invariably leads to loud and passionate infighting. After all, no male likes to be laughed at when he pulls his club out and then be told he doesn't have enough to get there.

SCOTCH MIXED FOURSOME*

A man and a woman pitted against another man and woman, with each couple alternating strokes until one of them holes out. We are obviously talking real debauchery here.

BINGO BANGO BONGO

The general idea of this little exercise in prurience is to try to be the first one on, closest to, and first one in! Enough said?

*Historical note: The name *Scotch Mixed Foursome* was derived not from the fact that indulgence in the activity will drive one to drink and dissipation—which, of course, it will—but rather from the ancestral heritage of the game itself. The explanation that has gained most acceptance is that many years ago an Englishman passing by a links in the Highlands saw two golfers taking turns hitting the same ball, playing two other golfers engaged in a similar practice. Not being able to tell if one of the two teams was his friend Robert and Robert's wife Robin and the other Robert's brother Roger and Robin's sister Rebecca, or if it was in fact a twosome of Robert and Roger against Robin and Rebecca—an understandable confusion since from a distance it was difficult to tell a man's kilt from a woman's skirt—the Englishman decided then and there that what he was witnessing was simply a Scotch Mixed Foursome. Let the kilts fall where they may!

THE NASSAU

The Nassau is without a doubt the most popular betting game used in match play. It can be used in everything from a singles match to a mixed four-ball.

Simply stated, the Nassau is a series of bets for $1 or $100—whatever amount you can't really afford to lose but would do anything to win—for each of three parts of the round: the front nine, the back nine, and the whole 18 holes. But in reality those three bets are just the come-on, the appetizer for the back-breaker, the infamous "press." Any number of presses can be in progress on top of the original bet. And God help the faint of heart and weak of putting stroke!

By adding "sandies" and "greenies" to the shenanigans, the cunning Nassau player will make sure to have so many bets going within the foursome that only his caddy can figure out who owes whom and how much when it's all over.

In fact, the betting can get so complicated that topflight caddies for Nassau betting usually moonlight as computer programmers. They don't come cheap, but a good one is worth his weight in Apples!

CHEATING

This is a very sore subject for hopeless golfaholics. Most problem golfers already have so much going against them that they would never in their right mind think of cheating.

But then most golfaholics haven't been in their right mind since anyone can remember! If they were, they wouldn't be golfaholics. Therefore, any reports of widespread cheating must be viewed with a certain amount of forgiveness and tolerance.

Now, of course, there are some truly demented afflictees who spend long, sleepless nights studying every rule and subrule in the book and can't wait to nail one of their foursome on some minute transgression. This maniacal policing of rules violations usually lasts until our vigilantes of truth and honor find themselves off by their lonesome and all set to bend a bothersome little twig—and Rule 17-1—only to be caught in the act by an even higher authority.

However, most golfaholics took one look at the Rules of Golf when they first plunged into the aberration and knew instinctively that if they ever took the time to understand every law and condition in the book—much less tried to play by them—they'd never finish a round of golf!

CAUGHT IN THE ACT BY AN EVEN HIGHER AUTHORITY

8

SIDE EFFECTS OF GOLFAHOLISM

One of the main reasons golfaholics would even consider bending the Rules of Golf when by themselves is because of what often happens to them when they have to make a shot with the whole world watching—actually just the rest of their foursome; it only seems like the whole world.

It is then, when the going gets tough—and it's big bucks that may be going—that golfaholics must come to grips with the two most potentially lethal side effects of their affliction. Of course we are speaking of nothing less than the unspeakable—choking and the yips.

CHOKING

Though the term *choking* would seem to describe a physical condition, in fact it is one of the psychological contractions most feared by golfaholics. To be sure, once one's mind is infected, the physical manifestations are truly hideous—an accident of nature of the most stomach-turning proportions.

Once golfaholics begin to choke the end is near. And the harder they try to stop choking, the worse it becomes, ultimately leading to chills, fever, bulging eyes, and heart-stopping cries of "OHHHHH, SHIT!"

THE YIPS

For years there has been an ongoing debate as to whether the *yips* is merely one manifestation of choking or it should stand alone at the top as the most excruciating psychomotor disturbance that every golfaholic is certain to contract sooner or later.

Whatever the final determination, there can be no argument that the yips attacks the nervous system when golfaholics are at their most vulnerable and pathetic: on short putts.

What golfaholic *hasn't* found himself starring in this scenario?

With no release of tension by waggling one's club or one's behind, coupled with the deathly silence of the rest of your foursome (who have already made their putts from much farther away and are licking their lips) and the thought that after 437 treacherous yards over water, sand, and trees all you have to do is roll that little ball into that tiny hole, which is so bloody close and yet so far—with all that stacked against you it is not surprising that you want to get the moment of truth over with so badly that either your trembling fingers "yip" the ball, which staggers aimlessly nowhere near the hole, a mere two feet away, or you freeze up in such paralytic cowardice that your caddy has to goose you with the cold head of your metal driver and you whack the ball 75 yards onto the next tee!

A PRAYER
FOR TIMES
OF STRESS

Now I lay my hands
    on putter
I pray the Lord my stroke
    won't stutter
If I should choke and yip
    and swear out
I pray the Lord won't yip
    my hair out!
And if my mouth needs more
    than washing
I give the Lord my soul
    for flushing.

9

THE MISSING LINKS

What we are concerned with here are the ever-widening voids in a life whose lust for golf, golf, and more golf overrides every other consideration for meaningful existence.

THE FIRST NINE HOLES

These are the vital missing links to a healthy connection with the real world.

Because of your blind obedience to golf:

1. You are not able to attend black-tie social events and converse intelligently on meaningful human values—other than Calvin Peete's driving percentage in the fairway and Morris Hatalsky's average putts per round.

THE MISSING LINKS

2. You have trouble enjoying the early formative years of your children's development without secretly wishing they'd hurry up and get big enough so they could caddy for you.

3. You never spend long, boring afternoons with visiting in-laws who only wanted your opinion as to some minor changes in their will. You didn't want to be bothered with all that blue-chip stock anyway.

4. You have never taken the time to cultivate proper social graces and etiquette. The boss's funeral is not the place to start replacing his divots. Nor does one tell his widow that the gravesite looks like "ground under repair" and suggest she allow the old guy a "free drop."

5. You never have the time to get involved in local civic organizations, giving of your energies and generously donating old golf clubs and spikes to community service clubs like the KKK.

6. You never put time aside for artistic expression. Classes in figure study have often helped satisfy the golfaholic's longing for the undulations of a favorite course. The rolling hills and valleys of this new layout may even stimulate a whole new game plan!

7. You don't make time for a disciplined physical fitness program. Unfortunately, playing 36 holes in a golf cart does not really qualify as meaningful cardiovascular exercise— no more than hitting your 2-iron over the 210-yard third hole can really be considered "pumping iron."

8. You never take the time to share the camaraderie of relatives and friends who have no interest in golf but prefer such pasttimes as bull-fighting, alligator wrestling, and climbing Mount St. Helens—just because it's still there!

   The fact is that the opportunity to experience a brush with death at the urging of a formerly close friend will make you realize how childish it is to be so terror-stricken of a little three-foot downhill, sidehill putt on a marble-slick green.

9. You are a real turkey by always spending Thanksgiving on the course, shooting hopelessly for eagles instead of being home and assured of getting the bird from everyone!

THE BACK NINE

These are the deeper chasms in a golfaholic's life. Commit any of the following and be prepared for the most dire consequences.

10. **You refuse to take the wife and kids on vacation to any place that doesn't have a golf course. Lord knows how many families of golfaholics will never get to Yellowstone until Pete Dye builds a great par 5 dogleg around Old Faithful. Or will never hike into the bowels of Carlsbad Caverns until they put in a nightlighted driving range. . . .**

    Or will never be allowed to gaze wondrously at Mount Rushmore until the U.S. government is willing to accord the same place in history to the likes of Bobby Jones, Arnold Palmer, Jack Nicklaus, and Orville Moody!

11. You are unable to stand back and see how destructive compulsive behavior can be. And how easily golfaholism can lead to other obsessions—hideous abnormalities such as:

> *Consumptive Hopscotchitis,* where the severely afflicted often refuse to begin hopping without a certain amount of preliminary Scotching.
> *Paralytic Ping-Pongemia,* which invariably leads to an intemperate yen for Chinese food!
> And the horrible *Dyspeptic Pistachiosis,* which is certain to drive you nuts or make you turn to advanced stages of Hopscotchitis.

12. You don't give serious thought to the adoption of higher business standards—not to be confused with adopting a higher handicap before an out-of-town game with corporate rivals.

13. You find yourself missing an IRS audit of last year's highly suspicious 10-to-1 leveraged tax shelter because of a last-minute invitation to play in the Spring Stag at the most exclusive golf club in town. And you made the right choice. After all, you won't get to play next year—you'll be in prison.

14. You never take time for any real soul searching. Who knows? You may actually have one!

15. You forget to encourage the daily living of the Golden Rule. However, "do unto others" does not mean nudging your opponent's ball into the water hazard simply because he nudged yours out of bounds.

16. You don't give primacy to human, rather than temporal, values; nor time to render altruistic patronage and high animism, which make possible the growth of moral rectitude, prudence, and patriotism!

17. You don't understand what the above means.

18. You are simply NEVER THERE!

Not being there when your first child was born and again on your daughter's wedding day and also on your son's graduation from West Point and at your wife's election to Congress because you just had to go those few extra holes can only be resolved by and must ultimately end in sudden death—when you least expect it.

And if a long reserved tee-time precludes you from making your own funeral, don't worry about it. No one else will be there either.

10

PORTRAIT OF A GOLFAHOLIC

In most cases the golfaholic was exposed to the affliction at a very early age. The child was taught to respect adults such as presidents who could often be seen on television slicing and hooking this way and that and generally teeing off on some poor soul during a golf tournament.

And yet, by the time our golfaholic went to college, he or she was still innocent enough to believe the old myth that playing golf could be an invaluable tool for future career advancement. The golfaholic was easily convinced that the kind of people one could meet and cultivate at the best golf clubs were a necessity in the hard climb up the corporate pyramid to riches and degradation.

After graduation our golfaholic generally began to spend less time at work and more on practicing pitches around aprons.

PORTRAIT OF A GOLFAHOLIC

Surprisingly, even with their over-heated swinging taking more of their time, most golfaholics were at one time extremely successful in business, medicine, science, education, religion, law, tax evasion, and politics before blowing it all on golf.

It is well known that ordinary golfers let the trials and tribulations of daily life affect their golf games.

Our golfaholic, however, takes it one step farther. He takes his agonies from the course back home to inflict on loved ones! One step in the door and the golfaholic will pour out heart and soul to children and spouses. Depending on the extent of his humiliation at the hands of the rest of the foursome—all cold-blooded hustlers and smiling sand-baggers—the golfaholic may babble on for hours alternating between uncontrollable weeping and hysterical laughter.

Fortunately, as years pass and the golfaholic matures, he or she usually tends to mellow. Agonies of days gone by are now remembered as glories of only last week. Our senior golfaholic may spend an hour deciding which golf cap to wear out to dinner. This is an important decision, particularly for family and friends accompanying the golfaholic, since the evening's conversation will center around every shot made on every hole on every course played by the golfaholic when wearing that particular cap.

A veteran golfaholic never forgets the truly important moments of his life.

A PRAYER FOR FORGIVENESS

Now I lay my hand
    to tee
My ball to hit in front
    of thee
If it should fly not
    of my choosing
I pray the Lord
    forgive my boozing
But should I quit
    give up my putter
My brain might dry out
    but my heart would sputter
It pains me Lord
    but be truthful I must
I'm a born-again golfaholic
    it's St. Andrews or bust!

PART II:

Golfaholics Anonymous—
The Answer
You've Been Swearing For!

11

WHAT IS GOLFAHOLICS ANONYMOUS?

It is a fellowship of men and women who have lost the ability to control their golfing and have found themselves in various kinds of traps and hazards as a result of their golf.

The sad truth is that most active golfaholics are not eager to cast off their tees and spikes simply because a loved one suggests it. Golfing habits are firmly rooted in one's personality, and real golfaholics are rarely ready, willing, or able to undergo the cure. For this they need the help and support of other golfaholics and GOLFAHOLICS ANONYMOUS.

. . . RARELY WILLING TO UNDERGO THE CURE

12

HOW DOES GOLFAHOLICS ANONYMOUS WORK?

One thing that almost all real golfaholics have in common is that, as time passes, their golfing gets worse. Oh, for a few brief shining moments their golf may somehow improve, but then, inexorably, the slide continues to dissolution, dissipation, and dominoes.

It is then that these chronic ball-beaters take pledges, make solemn promises, utter sacrilegious oaths, and throw away balls, bags, and bogeys—babies and bathwater may also be in jeopardy.

Golfaholics should now be good and ready for what we call *Cold Bogey*. This is the GOLFAHOLICS ANONYMOUS approach to rehabilitation and is based on the idea that every problem golfer, at one time or another, has gone for at least a week without a waggle.

A WEEK WITHOUT A WAGGLE

Yes, there are some who believe gradual withdrawal is a workable method of rehabilitation. Unfortunately, this method is successful with very few hardened golfaholics. The idea of cutting back from 18 holes to nine holes, and then to executive length courses, and then to par 3 layouts, and eventually back to miniature golf sounds easy, but in reality very few make it all the way back to the 18th tee on the miniature golf course and can stand by and watch as their ball disappears into that bottomless hole for the last time.

It was a shattering, gut-wrenching experience when they were kids and is just too emotionally overwhelming to have to go through again at this stage in life.

Gradual withdrawal and Cold Bogey not withstanding, the hard truth is that most of those who turn to GOLFAHOLICS ANONYMOUS are beyond hope. Often they need to be shipped off to Bismarck, North Dakota, for the winter and may emerge in the spring still shaking and unsure of what has happened to them. Their loved ones musn't be alarmed by how they look. Appearances can be deceiving. Anyway, pneumonia is a small price to pay when trying to control golfaholics' madness.

In all probability it will be a long, never-ending road to recovery. A golfaholic's compulsion to hack away his life is not easily deterred. For most it is a life sentence—or 50,000 rounds, whichever comes first.

13
GOLF SUBSTITUTES

During the endless rehabilitation process it is common for golfaholics to demonstrate energetic enthusiasm for golf substitutes. As a recovering golfaholic, you might be surprised to find yourself in intense pursuit of bookmaking, smuggling aliens across the border, managing lady mud wrestlers, and other long-delayed career goals.

Each of the following substitutes has something particular to offer you though it will undoubtedly take overindulgence in several of them to relieve the agonies of going Cold Bogey.

1. **Beating Your Head against a Hard Wall**—A simple and extremely effective golf substitute. Anytime you get the urge to golf, instead take 18 minutes and beat your head against a good solid wall! This is guaranteed to duplicate to a tee the physical and emotional beating you would have suffered playing a round of golf. If 18 minutes aren't enough, go for 27 or 36—whatever feels right.

2. **Smoking Cigars**—Guaranteed to preserve and maintain the low esteem family and friends already hold you in. You are assured of receiving the same ignominious glares when you light up as when you teed off.

3. **Selling Defective Arms to Third World Countries**—This should fill your desire for excitement, adventure, and the underlying terror that everything just might blow up in your face before the game is up.

4. **Training Llamas**—A particularly well-suited golf substitute since llamas can be playful, benign, and your best friend one minute and then for no apparent good reason spit in your eye and kick you in the ass. In these two respects you'll feel like you've just played a round on your favorite golf course.

Don't expect miracles!

It is entirely possible that none of the aforementioned substitutes will be enough. Should that be the case, we have generally found that extensive root canal work of many weeks' duration has a tendency to replace golf in one's mind.

Acute appendicitis accompanied by severe peritonitis also works wonders in separating you from your appointed rounds.

It might pay in the long run to sit down with your family dentist and surgeon and see what operations are open to you. Use your imagination. Get creative!

When it comes to chronic golfaholism, never forget that the end justifies the means.

For in your confused and double-bogeyed mind the need to navigate a small ball into a small hole with implements ill-suited for the purpose may truly be a matter of life and death. In fact, most die-hard golfaholics would rather suffer a stroke than be penalized one!

14
POSITIVE REINFORCEMENT

If golfaholics are to have any chance of returning to a normal, boring life, it is absolutely critical that they receive positive reinforcement from family and friends.

Once they no longer have golf as an outlet for the pressures of business and personal conflicts, they should be encouraged and praised for keeping everything bottled up inside like the rest of us. Show them how proud you are of how uptight they've become since putting golf out of their life.

And if their face breaks out in postadolescent zits or if unrelieved tension leads to dandruff, fever blisters, or a good old-fashioned ulcer, then don't hesitate to give them a real pat on the back and let them know how you feel.

And if what used to be a "lost weekend" with golf is now lost in front of the television playing Donky Kong like a zombie, then rejoice! For your golfaholic is back in the real world of mind-stupefying, juvenile, computer-dependent recreation.

POSITIVE REINFORCEMENT

And if home video games lead to a new fascination with all that television has to offer, be sure to give them three cheers when they come home with three new TVs for the bedroom, bath, and kitchen!

Stand behind them when they become infatuated with Julia Child. Tell them how great those 30 extra pounds of cholesterol look since French cooking became their passion. Don't be afraid to let them know you are with them all the way. Put on 35 pounds and get a leg up on arteriosclerosis!

Be sure to let them know you understand completely that all great chefs are tyrannical, insensitive, abusive, and impossible to live with, and you don't mind in the least being barred from the kitchen except when it's your turn to spend two hours cleaning up the mess they've created.

And be sure to take full responsibility for their attempted suicide. They had good reason to end it all by your cruel and thoughtless remark that their Coq Au Vin à la Bourguignonne reminded you a lot of McDonald's Chicken McNuggets.

Positive reinforcement! But be prepared: golf may be the least of your worries.

A PRAYER FOR POSITIVE REINFORCEMENT

Now I forsake my golfaholism
    for others
For this ism and that ism
    I need help Dr. Brothers!
And though family and friends
    keep on praising and thanking
In truth way down deep
    I'd rather be shanking
But if I should die
    without any more duffing
I pray God will know
    I'm still hooked

(Not really! Just bluffing)

15

YOUR OWN LIFE

If you are a normal golfer, you may wonder what to do about your occasional urge to play now that the golfaholic in your life is no longer doing it.

Should you abstain completely?

Should you stop playing around with your local pro?

It probably goes without saying—but we'll say it anyway—that it would be wise to conduct any social swinging with a certain amount of discretion. For golfaholics generally have very short memories. They quickly forget what being a golfaholic means. They may even play again. A binge of 72 holes in a day is not uncommon—which is exactly why the golfaholic must be made to feel as guilty as hell for past golfing transgressions. A big dose of guilt can be a very healthy thing—just ask any mother who lives with her married son.

So by all means, lay on the guilt trip. Your golfaholic must understand in no uncertain terms that there is nothing wrong with you. You're okay. He's the screwed-up sicko!

A BINGE OF 72 HOLES IN A DAY

16

IN THE FINAL ANALYSIS

At some point in time all golfaholics must look at themselves and face the bottom line: the staggering heights to which their handicap has risen, which is directly responsible for the inhuman lows to which they have plunged.

There is little more that anyone else can do. You, yourself, have to make the choices. Hard choices, which only you, the golfaholic, in your blackest of hearts and slimiest of souls, can decide.

ARE YOU FINALLY PREPARED TO:

> face realities instead of always improving your lies?

> acknowledge that your trouble lies in the fact that you are a no-talent, uncoordinated duffer, rather than blaming the golf course for singling you out to wreak its vengeance upon?

> continue swinging wildly all over the countryside knowing full-well the penalties you'll have to pay when you get home?

HARD CHOICE FOR THE GOLFAHOLIC

> cultivate a religious commitment other than the belief that prayer on bended knee while lining up a crucial putt is the best time to catch His ear?

> become a real person instead of a wood-brained, iron-hearted, spike-souled splotch in the sewers of modern civilization?

If you are prepared to make the changes and do these things, then there is a special place for you in the Smithsonian museum.

If, on the other hand, you are not prepared to make these sacrifices, then all is irrevocably lost and you are sentenced to cold and wet starting times in this life and everlasting hotter than hell ones in the next.

That's the bad news. The good news is that you won't be alone! There are a few million more of us right behind you wishing to hell you'd stop screwing around and hit the damn ball!

GARY PATTERSON

17

OATH OF ALLEGIANCE

Yes, I am a golfaholic. And I don't care who knows it!

I have turned to GOLFAHOLICS ANONYMOUS so that I may share with others like me the thrill of victory over nongolfaholics and the exaltation of knowing now and forever that there is no such thing as a bad golfer, only a sick one!

I hereby pledge to the golfaholics before me, my fore-fathers and fore-mothers, that I will hereafter experience the passion, the ecstasy, the forbidden fruit of my affliction only with other golfaholics and members of GOLFAHOLICS ANONYMOUS.

In doing so I admit that I am powerless over my unrepentant ball-beating ways, and I will solemnly try for a week without a waggle. But in certain failure I will then only waggle in the company of other willing wagglers who have also waddled off the wagon.

And finally, I swear my allegiance to GOLFAHOLICS ANONYMOUS, whose guiding principle is simply to keep our sickness and its small pleasures to ourselves. After all, we wouldn't want the whole world to know what we've got going!

18

AN AUTHOR'S CONFESSION

I am a golfaholic. And I don't care who knows it!

GOLFAHOLICS ANONYMOUS was established for people like myself who have no false illusions about what they truly are.

To others like us we are anything but anonymous. We know who we are. We share the same agonies and exaltations. And not just that great shot in the Club Championship with friends watching and maybe a few dollars on the line. But also the utterly private moments playing alone on a weekday evening, pretending that the long pitch over the bunker is for the Open Championship—and even though there is absolutely no pressure, no one watching, nothing to win or lose, you hit the shot with all the confident skill of Watson on the 17th at Pebble and watch as the ball rolls perfectly toward the flag, hits, and drops. And your heart sings and your face grins, and your eyes dance as you high-step toward the hole, raise your fist in victory, and say just loud enough for you to hear—actually hear your own voice say—"Now *that* was a great shot!" to which you can't help but reply to yourself, "You're damn right it was!"

The Duffers Series

The Official Duffer's Rules of Golf
John Noble
Illustrations by Tracy Butler
Golfing lore and terminology, etiquette on the course and what to do when hit by a golf ball. . . John Noble advises on all aspects of the game and introduces you to golfing types such as the hacker, the novice, the scratch player, the gambler and the pro.

The Official Duffer's Rules of Tennis
Bob Adams
Illustrations by Tracy Butler
The tennis duffer might not make Wimbledon, but he can make a name for himself in other ways. Bob Adams explains the finer points of duffers' play, their original attitudes to scoring, their best tactics for coming out on top despite formidable competition and a host of other arcane subterfuges.

The Duffer's Guide to Rugby
Gren
Introduction by Max Boyce
From the referee who got a new whistle for Christmas to such well-known playing types as the chap-who-happened-to-be-around-when-they-were-short, Gren brings to life an amazing gallery of all-too-familiar sporting heroes. He also provides invaluable advice on tactics ('It worked all right on the blackboard'), referees' signals (such as 'I want to go to the loo'), correct apparel, club people, playing positions, passes — and understanding the commentator.

The Duffer's Guide to Golf: A Second Slice
Gren
The popular Welsh cartoonist turns his attention from rugby clubs to golf clubs – those you drink in and those you hit balls with. He warns readers about the Sunday golfer who potters around the course as if he were gardening, the sales-manager type who only plays when a business deal is at stake, and the club drunk who can't remember why he's on the course at all.

The Duffer's Guide to Cricket
Gren
If the last time you bowled a maiden over was when your leg was before the wicket and you suffered a silly mid-on as a consequence, Gren's introduction to the world of cricketing types, field behaviour, bats, boxes and balls is the book for you.

The Duffer's Guide to Coarse Fishing
Mike Gordon
Introduction by Mike Harding
How to be a happy hooker in a few easy lessons: Mike Gordon takes you into the maggot-ridden world of tackle boxes and waders, discusses the comparative virtues of the stiff, the limp and the collapsible rod and reveals the meanings of trade jargon such as 'dry flies' (managing to keep out of the water) and 'breaking strain' (the point you reach when the weather becomes unbearable).

The Duffer's Guide to Spain
Gren
Wall-to-wall sangria, jellyfish rash and Montezuma's revenge. . . just some of the delights awaiting the unsuspecting duffer en route for Spain.

The Duffer's Guide to Greece
Gren
Dedicated to all those who think the Acropolis will be lovely when it's finished and that *souvlakia* is that funny dance Greek men do.

Available from all bookshops